A Selection of Poems
By Chuan Sha

Original Chinese by Chuan Sha

English Translation by Hong Liu

 Bestview Scholars Publishing

A SELECTION OF POEMS BY CHUAN SHA

Original Chinese by Chuan Sha
English Translation by Hong Liu

Copyright © 2019 by Bestview Scholars Publishing Limited. All rights reserved. Except by a reviewer who may quote passages in a literary review, no part in this book may be reproduced, transmitted, or stored, posted on or downloaded from the internet, without prior written permission from the publisher, whatever the reason and purpose may be, in any form by any means now known or yet to be invented.

ISBN: 978-1-896848-17-4

Bestview Scholars Publishing Ltd.
28 Briarglen Crt, Unit B.
Toronto, ON
M1W 3Z7
Canada
Email all enquiries to: **bestviewscholars@gmail.com**

Amazon.com is the distributor of this book. To maximize savings, **please order copies of this book directly from Amazon.com**.

Cover Design: Alice W. Huang
English Translation Editor: Freeman J. Wong

The author's views and opinions in this book do not necessarily represent those of the publisher.

Foreword: Introducing the Poet

Chuan Sha is an excellent poet I know;
Besides fine poems, he writes novels and plays.
His "Skirts" poems have been staged show after show;
His artistry radiates with dazzling rays.

A rare Canadian, he writes in Chinese,
Lives a simple life whose days are well spent;
He'd make do with jam and bread without cheese,
But writing forever makes him content.

I am thrilled his poetry book has come out;
I hope the reader finds it a good buy.
I treasure all his fine poems without doubt;
When you have read them yourself you'll know why.

May you love his poems as much as I do,
And like him as a writer and poet too.

Harry J. Huang[1]
2019

---

[1] Harry J. Huang, PhD, is a retired English professor in Toronto who has a long list of publications. He is also a translation scholar, a fiction writer, and a highly regarded translator who has translated into English an anthology trilogy comprising 293 Chinese short-short stories—masterpieces of over 160 Chinese short-short story writers in mainland China, Hong Kong, Macao, and Taiwan, among other literary works. The trilogy (Bestview Scholars Publishing, June 2019) includes:
- *A New Anthology of Chinese Short-Short Stories: Ancient and Contemporary Romance, Social Ills, Twists and Turns in Life,*
- *A New Anthology of Chinese Short-Short Stories: Satire, Love and Marriage,* and
- *A New Anthology of Chinese Short-Short Stories: Surprises, Wisdom and Philosophy.*

CONTENTS

Foreword

Blue Skirt   9

Red Skirt   10

Silver Skirt   12

Green Skirt   14

Black Skirt   16

Golden Skirt   19

White Skirt   21

Goodbye   28

Once   30

A Woman's Body   32

Seaside Cabin   35

Feminine Light   37

Night Song   39

Cries at Midnight   41

Flower Branches   43

The Eye of Spring   44

The River Has Risen   46

Deep Sleep   48

Sunset 51

March Wind 53

Sleeping Daffodils 54

Spring Night 55

Pink Beauty 57

The Night Behind You 58

Autumn Wind from Dye Lake 59

Boat Song 61

Flower 64

Evening Star 65

Say "Kiss" 66

Midland RT Station 68

Ocean 70

Light Mist 73

The Flag Bearer 75

Tomb Fire 77

The Wolves Are Howling 79

The Mountain Ghost Sings 80

A Target for Archery 82

Purple Flame in the Sky 84

Silence of the Master Poet 86

Dragonflies 88

Human Skin 90

Drumbeats Over the Snowy Ground 91

From the Land of Sinim 93

God's Hands 95

Hold My Hands 97

The Sea Beyond the Wall   100
There But Not There: The Muses by Zhao Yi-heng   102
Acknowledgements by Chuan Sha   104
Chuan Sha's Literary Career   106

Blue Skirt

The blue skirt
covers the woman, who feels
the passion of the sea.
An irresistible, trembling desire is felt,
as if it were a pack of hungry wolves.
Stares and gazes that are like waves
rush towards the woman's body.

The wind begins to moan,
and blows up
the skirt.
Choked with a deeper, further, and wider thirst,
The wolves watch the blue skirt being blown
rustling, into the distance
over the sea.

Red Skirt

Oh, my lady in
the red skirt!
You are the dream
that haunts the poet,
a flower that blooms
in the light
on the stage.
You are the first line of lyrics ever written,
the last note ever sung in an opera.
You are the water in an autumn lake
the bottom of which the fish swim.
You have seized us all,
and seized the light of
the world.
You are the water in a brook,
clean water that flows
through my cupped fingers.
You are a song from the mountain
where birds sing and soar

and trees crane up their heads
to listen.
There you are, in the red petals,
the white anthers,
the black sepals.
Flying overhead,
you fall gently
into a dream,
into a river that runs through the land,
sparkling in the sun,
with numerous men's eyes afloat.
Oh, my lady,
my lady in the red skirt,
you are the dream
that haunts the poet.

Silver Skirt

The skirt is silver,
and the lady is silver
in the silver skirt.
In the dark night,
she knits,
and she hums a childhood song.
In the song she finds herself dying,
and then reborn.
In the singing she is singing and disappearing,
and she is happy and sad.
Fingertips of the moon
play about as if in a dance,
the stars are knitted, one after another,
into the sweet dreams of her son.
Moonlight flows through her life loom,
turning a silver corner of her skirt,
into a new coat for him.

The skirt is silver,

and the lady is silver
in the silver skirt.
At dawn
she is waiting,
waiting for her son,
her golden son,
her son of gold—
her Sun.

Green Skirt

Green Skirt,
the lady in the green skirt,
you are the fields and the forest,
abundant and rich,
with clusters of fruits hanging from trees.
Moonlight flows in after sunset,
and sees the love banquet
where you cover your man,
cover the land and the forest.
The fields are burning
in your promise.
In the depths of the night,
the fire shoots into the sky.
You are the fire of the fire,
fire of the land,
fire of the rocks and stones
fire under the water, and
the fire that burns inside your man!
You a fire spirit

hidden inside
the green skirt.

It is autumn when
fruits hang from the trees,
and the animals sing in chorus.
Oh, lady
in the green skirt,
you are green
singing
a green song
joyful, proud, and
intoxicated,
in the green,
by your own amorous instinct.
Rejoicing and worrying,
you wonder if the day will come,
when the volcano erupts.
In front of you there is a silent door,
you are outside of it.

Black Skirt

Oh, the lady in black,
in the black skirt,
in the black veil that covers all
but your eyes,
eyes like precious stones, reflecting
your thirst.
The deep sea
has taken the lives of many men,
and buried their chilly white bones
in its fathomless bottom.
On the night of the full moon,
your tree rises through the surface of the sea,
and the bones put on flesh, then clothes, and gather atop.
The wild dancer among them is you.
Naked without the skirt of the ocean,
your body looks all white,
as you hold the moon in your mouth.

You are Cleopatra of the Nile,

whose nose draws the map of history on a coin.
You are a siren of the Mediterranean,
whose songs lure sailors to their death.
You are a goddess of the Aegean Sea,
whose stare brings the warriors to their knees under your skirt.
You are the priestess of Apollo,
whose wisdom makes all men fools.

It is only at night
when your songs are clear and piercing,
that birds fly into your cage.
That black and sensual palace of music, your cage,
where fine black wine is served,
and a black flower,
with a lethal fragrance
crawls into
bed
in the dark night,
whispering into her lover's ears,
while trembling,
and fully open.
Oh, you sit in front of a mirror,
appreciating every move you make.
Black Skirt,
the lady in the black skirt,
in the black veil that covers all

but that pair of eyes,
which like precious stones
bring forth the dawn,
and the sun that rolls up
from the surface of the sea.

Golden Skirt

Oh, the lady in the golden skirt,
the lady in gold,
the lady of gold,
she is the wife of a farmer,
a daughter and the daughter of a mother,
a daughter and the mother of a mother,
the daughter of the river,
the mother of ancient times.
She is in the mountain,
in the river,
on the high, high wind.
She is in the dream, galloping with her man on a white horse,
singing an old folksong.

She dreams of her man who had buried her a thousand times,
who died long ago.
She walks on the fields, where flowers bloom and wither,
through the villages where cooking smoke rises.

She bathes in the brooks,
and litters her way with precious stones.
Oh, the lady in the golden skirt,
the lady in gold,
the lady of gold,
she walks from sunrise
to sunset,
from dawn
to dusk.
She pauses atop the hills,
and waves goodbye
to the girl who follows her,
saying she alone will walk
through the sea of night.

On the other side of the night
stands a lady
in a silver skirt,
her mother,
who holds a rainbow skirt,
waiting for the day
to come.
After a bath in the sea of night,
she holds to her bosom the cotton clothes
for her baby girl,
in mixed colors,
the colors of Spring.

White Skirt

1

The white skirt,
worn by my lady, makes her
covered in white.
Oh, lady of the day,
the sun,
and the moon,
You are core of the fire,
a silver-white fire that seeks the truth of color.
Feelings of love
flash in your eyes,
female murmurs escape your cherry lips.
Your beautiful arms,
your holy pure, marble-white face, neck, and full breasts,
remind me, lady, of the amazing pieces of china
produced in the Yuan and Qing Dynasties;
you remind me of the holy body of Guan Yin[1]

---

[1] Guan Yin: Goddess of Mercy.

and of a ripe, juicy fruit hanging from a tree.
Your feminine fire, joined with spectrums,
licks the shadows, seductively, from your matured self,
and burns inside your soul and virginity.
You are the fire
that burns all
of your lovers.

2

Your lover, my lady,
is poetry,
is a poet,
male poetry,
a male poet—a male flower radiating with a golden rays.
Your lover is the land, the ocean, the sky, the sun, and Man,
the man of men and poet in the kingdom of poets.
You find him in a statue from the Mediterranean,
in fresco paintings of Dunhuang, Mt. Gu Yin and Harlong Valley,
in the forests of Georgia, Poland, Hungary
by River Don,
a warrior on a golden horse, or a silver one, or a marble one,
a Khan of Mongolia who aims his fully drawn bow
at a flying eagle.
Oh, my lady, your man gallops

from yesterday to today, to tomorrow,
from dusk to dawn,
from the edge of the grassland to the edge of the sky,
and he ponders.
Oh, my lady,
your lover is from the thread-bound books,
a witness of the chessboard war between Liu Bang and Xiang Yu
at Crane Ditch in the West Han Dynasty,
a General Xiang who groans in his concubine's arms defeated in a battle.
Oh, my lady,
your lover is a Chinese scholar dressed in a long gown, a silk cap,
wandering about in the 21st-century Europe,
daydreaming of a horseback fight among skyscrapers.

3

The white skirt,
by my lady, covers her
in white.
Oh, lady of the day,
the sun,
and the moon,
you are the land
the sea,
the sky!

Indeed, you are,
you are the land, the sea, and the sky;
you are the green grass in spring,
the colorful world of summer,
the animals in the deep forests,
a two-legged being in the city and countryside.
You are everything
that belongs to
the sun,
that is under the sun.
You are everything
that is under the moon,
that makes a man's life.
You are a man's moon at night,
the soul and spirit
that drag him around at night
when he looks through the mirror at
the unpredictable changes on screen of the night sky.

4

The white skirt,
of my lady, covers her
in white.
Oh, lady of the day,
the sun,

and the moon.

You are the beauty of the sea,

you are the rising moon that plays with the fragments of the sunset on the sea,

you are the setting moon that combs coquettishly in the mirror of the rising sun.

You are fair, charming, and infinitely beautiful,

you are a door between the sun and the moon,

you turn your back to them, the stars, and the eyes

that you face, meet and swallow.

You carry on your back a basket, as empty as your years,

that you use to catch the moon floating on the water.

Your eyes

are like those of an ancient Roman statue lost in thoughts,

one open and one closed,

one in the dark and one in the light,

both with tears of happiness and sadness.

Oh, your eyes, my lady,

when can they become like those of Venus of ancient Greece, who

tossed her head at the sun?

When can they open

with joy and charm?

5

The white skirt,

of my lady, covers her

in white.

Oh, lady of the day,

the sun,

and the moon,

you are a pearl-white beauty.

In a summer night, the moonlit fog dampens the fields,

at dawn the sound of a song pierces the rosy mist,

over the desert, the grassland, the forest, to where the water and the sky meet.

Over laughter and tears, both bitter and sweet.

A naked mountain ghost drags a leopard off the hills,

singing all the way.

That's all you have become at night, lady,

in your man's arms,

a dreamy weaving girl.

6

The white skirt,

of my lady, covers her

in white.

Oh, lady of the day,

the sun,

and the moon,

you dream of your lover.

The skirt, the flesh, and white whispers,

you are Venus,

truly.

You are a lily,

white with splendor,

listening in the dark to a poet's song.

Shaking and shifting, lady, you find yourself in the midsummer night,

flying, and flying,

toward the sky

full of stars.

Goodbye

Goodbye, causal and quick,
in a peaceful morning, in a foggy dusk,
to a ship ready to set sail,
beside a train starting to move on the flashing rails,
to the figure receding at
the entrance to the village.

Goodbye, most of the time,
in tears,
in cries
that you've heard,
that you've seen.

Goodbye, you would say to a friend,
who, after a life of noise and vigor,
closed his eyes on the world.
The iron doors of the crematory close,
the tomb stands, the moss clings,
clings to the epitaph of the tomb.

Purple flowers are dotting the field
of the pure bright spring.
They whisper in your ears
how the folks pray for you,
from the other side of the ocean
at the dawning of the day.

Once

Once
there was love as sweet as candy,
in a dance on a glass floor
in poetic innocence.
Tragedy came when adults took control,
the heart became sullen,
the voice frozen
like a piece of fossil.

Once
there was a single Er-hu
soloing the night rain into the top of Mt. Ba.
At the crossroad, a street lamp sputtered,
pulling the shade of red oiled-paper umbrellas
to a remote corner of the lane.
Falling rain had a rhythm on the stone steps,
in the autumn pond, a choir refreshing
the memory of the mossy green pebbles.

Once
there was the ancient bamboo raft of time,
on the noisy river,
floating downstream to a flowery road's end.
Then your hair combed in bangs,
you gazed with black glowing eyes
at the water pushing the raft toward the East.

A Woman's Body

A woman's body, as beautiful
as the ridges and grooves of a coin.
In the past,
one body after another
was drowned in the clear water of the sea,
with leaves, branches, roots, and soil,
drowning in fragrance of the air.
On the stage of night,
flapping her wings,
every single
flower –
red,
yellow,
blue,
purple,
white,
yearned to fly.

Time passes.

In the sea there is only you,
and you alone, who
swim to the shore,
in a wintry night
in the moonlight.
Feathers turning to scales,
you are still formed as human, naked,
as the one on the rock in Copenhagen.

In a London bookstore near Piccadilly Circus
Jupiter shoots his arrow into a photo album that
unfolds a thrilling view
at nightfall.
A thousand nudes creep out of photography history,
dancing, twisting, flirting,
climbing the totem pole
of the phallus,
until the first glimpse
of daylight.

Yet it's only you,
your naked beauty,
that's fit
for print.
My physical self
with my soul
is lit up

like a white bulb that
explodes, and is
scattered in the endless night,
over the tombs.
We lock ourselves in kisses
by the shore on a wintry night,
in the moonlight.

Seaside Cabin

The cabin stands by the sea,
separated by a thick wall of winds.
Waking up from my dream,
I seem to hear
from the other side
my love
fumbling
in her room to
undress.
Minutes later,
nothing
is audible but the sound
of the sea.

The cabin stands by the sea,
separated by a thick wall of winds.
Waking up from my dream,
I seem to see
my love sitting

upon the water,
undressed.
My thoughts, like the ridges and the grooves of fingers,
pile up a fall of water that
washes the grass juice
off her naked back.

The cabin stands by the sea,
separated by a thick wall of dreams.
Every inch of the roof
is covered with red vines,
whose leaves
point to
the other side of the sea.
Midnight brings in
the sound of musical waves,
I hum with the song that comes up to me
from the bottom of
the ocean.

Feminine Light

for Y.Y.

Feminine light,

your feminine light,

your choking feminine light,

your prairie wolf's feminine light.

Your feminine light

shines over my window that faces

a thousand-year-old broken wall,

shines upon my weather-beaten face,

and into my shattered dream of a previous existence,

where it freezes the fossil of my body.

Your fur, soft and silky, weeps in the light

growing all over the cracks of my rocks.

So, your feminine light smells of the prairie wolf's fragrance, so, you are such a gentle, loving female wolf

whose sharp teeth are tearing at my fossil heart

from which fresh blood keeps dripping

onto the ground.

Night Song

The night song begins to rise,
in spring
from the narrow streets,
from the eaves of the houses,
from the gilt frames of windows.
When a canvas painting is split open,
she stands there!
Her long, black hair
tumbling like a waterfall
onto her bare back,
singing back to
the night song,
she follows
the mermaid
into the depths of the sea,
singing and singing
on, and
on . . .

The night song rises,
in spring
from the night mountains and fields.
Following the mountain ghost's steps
she climbs up a plum tree,
naked, delicate,
amorous, pure,
rivaling the moon and the flowers.
She wanders as a lovely nude
about the hills.
The mountain ghost is frightened of humans
but how can she sing
so wonderfully
a night song?
She sings and sings,
on, and
on . . .

Cries at Midnight

Cries are heard at midnight
from the end of the corridor.
Is that a boy locked inside,
home alone?
The cries are loud, and
continuous.

Cries are heard at midnight
from the wildness of the land.
Is that an old wolf,
whose eyes flash with hunger?
The cries are loud, and
continuous.

Cries are heard at midnight
from the sky.
Is that a lost bird
trying to catch up with time?
The cries are loud, and

continuous.

Cries are heard at midnight
from around the tombs in the barren suburb.
Is that a lonely spirit
who waits for his loved ones?
The cries are loud, and
continuous.

Flower Branches

for Y.Y.

The flowery branch stands out,
just open in my broken eyes.
It stands out in the early spring of March,
green against the cracked fields.
When the cold sweeps over
with the shadow of death,
when things fall apart,
it sways, reaching upward to the sky.

The Eye of Spring

for Y.Y.

Spring eyes,
a shy and charming lady,
with spring eyes,
beams in the light of the season,
reflecting my lonely sky.

Gray winter
sees the black piano top open quietly amongst the scattered floating clouds.
The silvery keys glisten, on which
a lady's delicate fingers dance.
A naked statue seems to move in the air,
and black flower stems, bloom from a pale music sheet.
They groan together,
singing a song of flesh,
singing,
singing, and
singing,

singing of the warm night,
singing of tomorrow's rising sun,
singing of my summer to come.

The River Has Risen

—From Firth of Forth, Edinburgh to
hometown's Flower Stream River

The river rose up
in the spring night,
the raindrops beating the surface of the water.
"Don't go back!" he said,
"Don't go back!" she said,
"Hold tight, tighter!" they said.
Flashing waves crashed toward the shore,
the water, sloshing, rose above their ankles.

The river rose up
in the summer night,
the thunder rumbled across the sky.
Trees were struck to a flame on the hill,
Scared dogs kept on barking.
"Don't go back!" he said,
"Don't go back!" she said,
"Hold tight, tighter!" they said.
Flashing waves crashed toward the shore,

the river water, sloshing, rose above their chests.

The sea rose up
in the autumn night,
the raindrops beating the surface of the water.
The thunder rumbled no more in the sky,
the trees were no longer aflame on the hill,
the dogs were no longer barking in their hometown.
"Don't go back!" he said,
"Don't go back!" she said,
"Hold tight, tighter!" they said.
Flashing waves crashed toward the shore,
the sea water, sloshing, rose above their ankles.

"Don't go back!" she said,
 "Hold tight, tighter!" she said.

Then, a moonlit road appeared
on the quiet surface of the sea.
There came
a woman.

Deep Sleep

for Y.Y.

You've fallen into a
deep sleep,
I look at you
and kiss you, yet
am I in a dream?

Ivory lines float over
your beautiful body,
your loose hair pours like a waterfall
down till it joins with the white sun.
You eyes are closed, your lashes long and beautiful,
locking your naughty nature in
with your dreams.
What a mask of peace,
and of charm!
Surprised?
Reproaching?
Disappointed?

Fearless?
Your chin tilts upward; your cherry lips mutter;
the beautiful hairy flower blooming in
your groin seems to say,
death is not in yet,
life doesn't have an end,
why don't we enjoy this moment
on the doorway between life and death?

Here I kiss you,
kiss . . .,
my dear delicate love,
on your closed eyes,
your dream gate.
Your vacant eyes belong to a stone statue
that has long sunk into the depths of the ocean,
looking back from the other end of life,
through the fate that stands between the sea
and the sky,
and the sound of
snoring.

A deep sleep
you are in a deep sleep,
and I am terrified,
terrified at being separated from the world.
I kiss you,

I keep kissing you,
while my mind flies to heaven,
till daybreak when the sun rises.

Sunset

The sun is setting.
At sunset
I feel homesick.
The golden rays spread toward the east,
the east where the trees
cast their shadows,
the east which is the bright part
of the land.
The east is
my home.
The sun is setting.
At sunset
I feel homesick.

The sun is setting.
At sunset
I feel sad.
It sets off rays,
the rays of gold, like those that

flash in my mother's eyes.
The sunlight will disappear; then
Mother will leave me and
walk into the dark night.
The sun is setting.
At sunset
I feel sad.

March Wind

The March wind
sweeps the dust
off the windows,
and touches the little white flowers
under the dirty slush of melting snow
over the vast Canadian fields.

At night,
the moon shines.
Over the Pacific Ocean
the sounds of hand drums
and bell drums resound like waves.
The blade of the Er-hu
cuts in an opened wound,
playing with
the broken strings of
an ancient harp.

Sleeping Daffodils

The sleeping daffodil
dreams peacefully
in the autumn wind,
awakening, in someone's dream.

The sleeping daffodil
dreams peacefully
in the spring breeze,
awakening, in my dream.

The sleeping daffodil
dreams peacefully
in a dream of a dreamer,
always, in my dream.

Spring Night

Spring night,
waves charge, aiming for the sky,
and rush towards the window that faces the dark.
Your maiden hair looks as if washed by the night;
your eyes shiny, your teeth pearly,
your red long skirt dances in the wind.
I find my eyes unfocused
before the rosy branches that your laughter clings to,
beneath the indigo sky where stars hang,
on this spring night.

Spring night
is the time that
we sing songs,
and drink wine.
We shower in the open air,
listening to the turtledoves cooing in the valley,
insects chirruping in the grass, and
fish and shrimps singing in the brooks.

They cry happily
when they mate and play: the crabs, turtles,
crocodiles, frogs, and salamanders . . .

Why do we need summer,
autumn, and winter,
which all fly like an arrow?
What follows the sprout is the flower, then the fruit,
then its death, and back to the sprout!
After the sprout is the flower, then the fruit,
then its death and back to the sprout again!

Spring night
is the time that
we sing songs,
and drink wine.
We play with
the strings that make
a web of the spring night.

Pink Beauty

Pink Beauty
in the sun,
hides in the vapor of
the curling steam,
and is heard
from the buzzing of the bees.
Oh, Pink Beauty,
you sleep on the green leaves of summer.

Pink Beauty
atop a candle,
dances in front of the
cameras,
her laughter
blooming like a flower.
Oh, Pink Beauty,
you huddle yourself in bed, naked.

The Night Behind You

You ask what I was looking at—
the night behind you.

You ask what I was looking at—
the chirping bird in the garden behind you.

You ask what I was really looking at—
the night and the chirping bird in the garden, behind you.

You ask what I saw—
you, the very night behind you.
You, the chirping bird in the garden behind you.

Autumn Wind from Dye Lake

Composed by Loch Ness

The autumn wind smells of Dye Lake,
oh, Dye Lake of my town!
The wind never smells of the deep Atlantic Ocean,
but of Dye Lake!
Dye Lake has no chilly current as does the Atlantic,
no creatures would raise their heads above the water there,
pitiably weeping at the moon: walleyes, rock bass,
rainbow trout, silver perches, and
flounder . . .

In the wind that smells of Dye Lake,
there are no fathomless blue eyes.
The flowing fragrance lingers of chrysanthemums,
of bamboos, and pines.
The mountain brooks meander pleasantly,
where silver carp, grass carp,
fish and frogs,
play and laugh,

full of noisy fun.

The autumn wind smells of Dye Lake,
oh, Dye Lake of my town!
The wind then kept blowing,
and there you stood by the lake!

You looked and smiled
just like Dye Lake in autumn,
the mirror-like water
rippling gently.
Raindrops hung on the flowers, the grass, and trees;
the tears dripped down your cheeks, into the brook, into the lake;
your lips matched the maple leaves,
fallen upon the surface.
I found my face reflected, rippled in the clear, pure water,
found myself lost in the pine bushes of the silent mountain.

The autumn wind smells of Dye Lake,
oh, Dye Lake!
Tonight,
beyond the lake,
Robert Burns[1] might hear me
crying.

---

[1] Robert Burns (1759-1796): a Scottish poet.

Boat Song

A boat song,
the fishermen on the beach are singing a boat song.
"Tin-tin tong! Tin-tin tong!
Tin-tin tong tong, tin tong tong!
Go, brothers! Go, sisters,
Move your limbs, your lips, your behinds . . .
Raise the axes, raise the saws, drive your wedges . . .
The bow should be sharp,
the stern should round,
the hull should be hollow,
the sail needs a strong wind . . . "

The men sing, men of different skins,
green,
yellow,
red,
black,
grey,
and freckled.

Everyone sings,

everyone sings from the pointed awning room in the belly of the boat,

They sing all seasons

to the sun,

to the moon,

against the wind,

in the rain,

from the beach to the sea.

"Tin-tin tong! Tin-tin tong!

Tin-tin tong tong, tin tong tong!

Go, brothers! Go, sisters,

Move your limbs, your lips, your behinds!

Raise the axes, raise the saws, drive your wedges . . .

The bow should be sharp,

the stern should round,

the hull should be hollow,

the sailboat needs a wind . . ."

The beach sings,

the wind sings,

the water sings,

the sea birds sing,

the fish sing,

human bones of different colors sing

from the bottom of the sea.

The song is gone now,
gone from the beach, the boat,
gone with the awning room that used to be
in the belly of the boat.

Flower

The flower shows off her color,
shaking off a fragrance
from a wet green branch,
to the wind,
and then withers without a sound.

The flower gives out light,
burning on the tip of a candle
against the night,
splendidly,
and then dies out without a sound.

The flower looks up to a bird,
fluttering among the trees in seasonal colors,
in the warmth of the land,
chirping sweetly in its glory,
and then rests in peace, covered by grass leaves without a
 sound.

Evening Star

for Y.Y.

The evening star,
star of my peaceful night,
twinkles as Venus, an eye catcher
in the ocean of stars.
The ocean above is so far away,
yet the fire burns, followed by
millions of stars that dart towards me,
a light of feminine fire!
Oh, the star, as clear and pure as crystal,
you shine on my remote past,
you shine on my remote future,
igniting the fire that burns all to ashes which
you hold in your bosom.

Say "Kiss"

Softly you said,
"Kiss," in the depths
of the night.
"Kiss . . ."
and again,
"Kiss . . ."

The moon, and
the stars,
were dwarfed
by your tender eyes,
pure and clear, that were
like a mountain spring.
Your eyes, so clear and soft,
were dwarfed
the moment you said the word,
"Kiss . . ."
It was not the charm of your slim figure,
your pure and smooth skin,

your smiling face,
or your bangs combed by the moonlight,
but the word you said in the dark
that held me captive.

There is no other woman
on this earth
that has given me
such a soft whisper:
"Kiss . . ."
That word:
"Kiss . . ."

Midland RT[1] Station

The sky train, at Midland RT Station, is departing.
Its gray doors close, locking in
your smile,
your long lashes,
your lovely face.
All is gone.
The willow branches,
swayed in the wind, wither
upon their past greenness.
The gray wooded fence
produces a dry, creaking sound that pounds
on the wooded frame of a mirror, on which
a sad gaze is frozen.

My love,
her face soft and delicate,
eyes like roses,

---
[1] RT: Rapid Transit, part of the subway in Scarborough, Ontario.

kisses my physical self.
Oh, my heart,
my eyes!
How many more nights of cynical life
will you go through
before you reach out
and kiss the daybreak that we strain to see
before we see death?

The sky train is departing,
its gray doors close.
you move on your crippled feet,
alone and soundless,
with my kisses,
toward the line of horizon.

Ocean

Ocean,
oh, Ocean!
You are a full-bodied beauty,
a coquettish blond with blue eyes,
born and bred in the cradle under the blue sky!
How did you manage to hide yourself
on the other side of the ranges of
mountains, the endless stretches of
forests, and beyond?
How were you able to hide yourself from me, with
lakes, rivers, and vast deserts, grasslands,
fields and fields over,
until I was old?

Ocean,
oh, Ocean!
You are such a full-bodied beauty,
such a coquettish blond with blue eyes!
Why didn't I meet you in my flourishing years,

when I was dressed in Tang gowns?
I could've fallen in love with you
on a starlit summer night, and
locked you in my arms, and
walked you through forests and forests
till we reached my village.
Or held you in my arms
and crossed lakes, streams, rivers, and oceans
till we reached my village on the other side.
Or carried you over deserts, grasslands, and vast fields
till we reached my village where poplars grew.
I'd have tossed you into the wheat field beside the threshing ground,
I'd have stripped you naked, locked you in my bosom,
and rolled with you on the threshing ground,
whining, crying, yelling,
in wild joy, tears, sweat,
with dust flying everywhere!
You would have given birth to sons and daughters,
Who'd all have one black eye and one blue, just like the sea,
and whose hair'd have been a mix of black and blond.
They would have stronger descendants,
generation after
generation . . .

Ocean,

oh, Ocean!

You are such a full-bodied beauty,

such a coquettish blond with blue eyes!

You are stout like a Scotland cow,

your marble neck, arms, full breasts, wide belly

and sensual buttocks and legs,

and every single part of your flesh,

is what I dream to possess,

dream to be intoxicated in, to lose myself in!

Light Mist

Here they come,
showered in the light mist,
girls laughing wholeheartedly.
They run out of the misty doors, one by one;
perched upon their heads
are little golden snakes that
huddle in groups, hissing.
These girls,
their eyes emitting flashes like lightning,
wear nothing, so as to uncover
their purely white bodies,
charming, shrouded
in the morning mist,
smelling of sunshine,
symbolizing the fairies
who gather.

On the left is St. Anna Gate
and on the right David Gate.

Remote and
beyond
is the waging blue sea that joins with
the end of the sky above
where Jesus Christ stands,
clothed in bark,
a glorious cross in hand,
pointing to the sun.
And
there comes
the clear and piercing
resounding of
bells . . .

The Flag Bearer

—To all historians

In the battlefield of history
the flag bearer fell down
slowly, silently, then
became ashes floating in the sunshine,
blown away to the darkening dusk,
to the halo of the moon, and
to the melted rocks and soil.
Little is known about him,
a blind spot that links to the past,
a blank page in the books.
In the dead of the night,
I open the thread-bound books passed down from my
    great-grandfather,
astounded at the woodlice, busy eating away at the
    pages,
the absurd symbols, crying so for the prejudiced that
their groans tear my lungs!

Over the piles of his comrades' corpses,
the soldier marched on, flag in hand,
toward the dawning of victory.
At daybreak as he was to hand the flag
to the eloquent speaker,
he fell at a shot heard from behind.
Knowing little what to say and how,
the flag bearer held the flag high,
and passed it into the hands of the speaker.
Nothing but a shadow in the sunshine,
he watched the speaker drag the blood-soaked flag away,
and sit in the emperor's gold throne!

Summer 1995
Pere-Lachaises Cemetery, Paris, France

Tomb Fire

—A prayer for Martyr Zhang Zhi-xin

A tomb fire,
the blue flame atop a grave at midnight.
It is a song, a poem by one that should not have died,
proving that spirits exist, spirits wrongfully treated.
The tomb fire, the truest history ever written, moves
in the forest of torches where justice lingers.
It burns to death whoever is doomed,
and leads to eternity whoever deserves it.
It burns on tips of little yellow flowers
over the land of spring,
and with bell-bellied fireflies that dance through the night,
pointing to the Mid-July Festival of Spirits,
brightening the Milky Way on which a full moon hangs.

Oh, listen with your heart!
Have you not heard
that the fire burns into a storm,

blowing at the curtain of the sky?
Oh, look with your eyes!
Have you not seen
that from the darkest corner of mankind
the fireball reflecting justice and conscience
is lifted by the blue splendor,
burning . . .

Summer 1995
Notre Dame, Paris, France

The Wolves Are Howling

—After the first reading of Jean Paul Sartre

The wolves are howling,
beyond the deep sea,
at the end of the wild land,
in a hunt for the flesh
of fish,
of beasts,
and for
human blood!

The wolves are howling,
savoring their meal,
with the tips of their sharp teeth,
the bones
of fish,
of beasts,
which excite their thousand-year long dream
to lick
a human heart!

The Mountain Ghost Sings

From the field comes the voice of a woman,
a song by a mountain ghost.
She sings her way out of the hills,
her arms open to the dark void
of the night,
shining with the purest of her
naked beauty.
She hugs the night,
embraces the darkest world,
a mountain ghost.
Human embraces are not like that,
as there exists no mountain ghost in the human world.

The mountain ghost sings on,
a female voice to meet daybreak.
She sings about the land,
just before the day dawns.
She sings for the people
who walk at night, and

those who she knows well—
the farmers, artisans,
tramps, or thieves—
the most miserable
in the human world.
To graves or heaven
they may go,
they remain her closest brothers and sisters.

Dawn hears the female's voice,
the mountain ghost's song.
The night is over,
the sun will be in to see
an evil, ugly
mankind.

A Target for Archery

—The Fate of A Tribe

The target
floats
in the air.
It is not a disciple of the Nazarene,
nor a pilgrim who walks to Mecca to listen to the
thinker who searches for solitude
on Mt. Hira before preaching about Allah,
and certainly nor a believer of Siddhartha Gautama.

Yet he is being shot.

Wailing, crying,
tearing lungs and hearts.
onlookers clap their hands and jump with joy,
watching the bows bend,
and the sharpened arrows, as they, one by one,
pierce him into the layers of darkness.

No one is aware
that everyone is a target,
a living target,
for someone else's aim,
floating
in the air.
Multi-god worshipers' descendants,
without their own godfathers,
are shooting him.
He is covered with wounds,
like a hedgehog in the bushes,
crying to himself before
finding joy and comfort, walking
through the three gates that divide thirty-six skies,
and reaching the Heavenly Court.
His soul travels out of his body,
over the Taoist rites,
free.

They are marching onto the shooting range,
floor after floor,
through all the thirty-six floors of Hell.
They are no more shooters,
but targets for archery
that float
in the air.

Purple Flame in the Sky

In the sky there is a flame
burning with a purple light,
sounds of hissing, licking, and cracking filling the air.
The fire—
it is red,
it is orange,
it is yellow,
it is green,
it is blue, and
it is purple that follows and lingers
after all the other colors die away.
Yes, it is a solid purple mass that burns
right after the red, orange, yellow, green, and blue extinguish.
It is a fire, an ultraviolet ray of fire,
the purest,
the warmest,
burning atop all city's high-rises
with a purple light.

Everything on top of the buildings,
every single bit,
has been burnt to nothing
beneath the sky,
all, except the steel racks left dangling,
and the parched corpses of the ants,
and tatters of clothing.
There! Out of the purple fire,
fly the naked angels
to the sky, the pure and clear sky
where the purple flames!
They are my sisters;
they fly with me.
While the elder sisters become younger ones,
the younger ones become infants.
Then I hear the blue sea
laughing, and see the
waves surging joyfully, kicking up white foam.
but those are my tears.

Silence of the Master Poet

The poet who strained his back to support
the sluice-gate
finally
dropped his empty bowl,
and walked out of the door,
leaving behind him a piece of land
littered with white bones.
He fell down at last
with the Island of the North Sea,
and the City that Gazed at the Sky,
and the Son of the Sea who took a train back to
the ancient land,
and the half Index Finger dancing in a lunatic house,
down, together, to the bottom of the sea,
with their thread-bound books.
They finally tempered that period of time
into pure gold, silver, and stone.
They succeeded,
yet they had left behind the pale sky

where the vultures soared, and
cursed loudly.
The living were willing to offer their flesh no more,
and the dead had no more bones to feed them with.
Above the horizon of the land
the sunlight felt like fire and looked like snow,
the scarecrows on the dry fields
cast away their hats
and crossed their legs, meditating,
then pounded their begging bowls.
Sparrows, crows, and buffaloes had been eaten,
the people hid as far as they could,
rocks and tiles were scared into the hills
while rice paddies, wells, and jars were driven to the river.
Inside the village,
the rows of tombs were crying
beneath the lonely sky.
The sound of an Er-hu rent the air, like a sword
cutting the Yangtze River
open to the bottom.
The bottom, where singers of the Red Songs
were reciting verses of
revolution.
Fish clothed in scales that shone like coins
swam by and disappeared.

Dragonflies

1

A dragonfly is what
I wish to be.
The huge
crystal clear eyes that can
look at the world from all sides.
I wish to have its wings,
its glimmering, translucent wings,
that glisten and dazzle,
so light and soft,
fully made,
made to carry me over in this world.

2

A red dragonfly,
a green dragonfly,
blue,
black,

white, or
even a spotted dragonfly.
Whereas I wish I were a red one,
God made me to be a black dragonfly.

3

Oh, the black dragonfly!
How I envy you!
Your icy clear eyes,
and your marvelous wings.
Yet God made me to be
a lonely
man!

Human Skin

The first time I see a man, I see a normal man.
The second time I see a red-skinned man,
the third time I see a white-skinned man,
the fourth time I see a brown-skinned man,
the fifth time I see a green-skinned man,
the sixth time I see a purple-skinned man,
the seventh time I see a black-skinned man,
the eighth time I see a mixed-skinned man,
the ninth time I see an animal-skinned man, and
the tenth time I see a normal man.

I see them all in the mirror.

Drumbeats Over the Snowy Ground

A building at the corner of a courtyard
at the intersection of Yonge and College Streets,
is covered by snow, pale against the dusk.
The chilly wind carries the sound of drumbeats,
drums of all sorts,
conga, kettledrums, and bongos,
played by hands, by sticks, with cymbals.
Tong, dar-dar, tong, tong!
tong, tong, tong, pang!
Tong, dar-dar, tong, tong!
Tong, tong, tong, pang!

Red caps, white caps, yellow caps
all rise and fall with the beat.
Hands and sticks dance in air,
passersby stop and crowd around,
the white, the black, the yellow, the mixed,

all clapping, stamping, puffing,
and singing.
Ah, ah, ah . . .
tong, dar-dar, tong, tong!
Tong, tong, tong, pang!
Tong, dar-dar, tong, tong!
Tong, tong, tong, pang!

Red caps, white caps, yellow caps,
all rise and fall, in tune with the drumbeats,
hands and sticks dance in air,
passersby stop and crowd around and dance.
The snow-covered ground is the surface of the drum,
the feet are the drumsticks,
weaving a rhythm that
hits home, the home
of the world.

The frozen world awakes, marveling at the scene,
and her pitiful eyes fill with
joyful tears, touched
by the beat of the happy drums.
Tong, dar-dar, tong, tong!
Tong, tong, tong, pang!
Tong, dar-dar, tong, tong!
Tong, tong, tong, pang!

From the Land of Sinim

"And these are from the land of Sinim."[1]
The night, at its darkest,
sees silver flashes
flying across
the waves,
and hears, with its mind, voices
sounding like fireflies, and
sounding like spirits from the seabed, all at once.

"And these are from the land of Sinim."
The night, at its darkest,
sees the silver flashes
flying across
the waves,
and sees, with its mind, an army of men wearing loose war robes,

---

[1] From Isaiah: 48:12. Some claim that major ancient civilization kingdoms referred "Sinim" to ancient China.

holding lanterns strung up to the sky.

"And these are from the land of Sinim."
The sun is shining over the fertile land
of Europe and North America,
over the African plain.
It filters through ranges of hills and gardens
on earth, seeing
the spots of fire that burn like
golden bouquets,
blooming in the splendor of roses and tulips.
These flowers, peonies,
red and magnificent,
are from the land of
Sinim!

Summer 1995
Strait of Dover, France

God's Hands

God's hands,
that master time,
one for the day, and one for the night.
When God works with His hands,
our calendar is turned over, page by page.

God's hands,
that master life,
one for death, and one for life.
When God works with His hands,
we are born and we die.

God's hands,
that master us humans,
one for man, and one for woman.
When God puts His hands together,
we have children.

God's hands,
that master human and beast.

When God works with the hand for the beast,
we are beast humans;
when God works with the hand for the human,
we are human beasts;
and when God works with His two hands,
we are humans.

God's hands,
masters of war and peace.
God plays the hand for peace when He is pleased,
and plays the hand for war if He is annoyed.
History comes to form in God's changeable mood.

God's hands,
He uses to cover His face with,
at seeing the living creatures.
He is too ordinary and too shabby,
wearing no fanciful garb, but clothing of tree bark.
Yet God's hands
hug all the creatures
when they die.
He looks at our charming faces as at His own,
knowing that He is unknown,
and that we humans are dirt,
are blind when we have eyes to see!

Hold My Hands

—On reading Nietzsche

Hold my hands
and flow
into my heart.

A choir is singing,
and the songs are like piles of waves
that rush forward.
When the curtain falls after the show,
the applause echoes like raindrops beating the banana leaves.
On the battlefield the bullets streak through my heart,
blinding lightning flashes across the sky and into the earth.
All this flows into,
ever into,
my heart.

Hold my hand,
and hold it tight!

Hold my heart,
my heart from which
tangling roots grow.
Your hands are so warm,
oh so warm.

Hold my hand,
and hold it tight!

You said
"The world is deep, shrouded by seven layers of loneliness."
You asked me
how many layers I had felt?
Does your light "belong to the remote world"?

I am scared,
yes I am,
that all at once the choir will stop singing,
the applause will stop,
the guns will cease to fire and all will be deadly quiet,
that the lightning will illuminate the raindrops falling to the earth;
I fear that moment.

The sea is calm, though, beneath the winter moon.
On the mirror-like water,

there is nothing but the singing from Dynebelle.[1]
One after another hands are released.
The only one left behind
is Dynebelle and her sentimental,
enchanting
songs.

I dream of the bottom of the sea,
and I see
only
my fingers,
while Dynebelle's songs
float over
the surface of the ocean.

---

[1] Dynebelle: an opera singer from Xingjiang, China.

The Sea Beyond the Wall

Beyond the wall is the sea
blue,
from light and dark,
stretching to
the endless sky.

Beyond the wall is the sea,
above the sea is the sky,
above the sky is sunshine,
further above is the sun.

Beyond the wall is the sea,
that is
all.

Beyond the wall is the sea,
yet how could you not
see it until this minute?

Beyond the wall is the sea,
listen,
and listen to the waves
crashing on the beach.

There But Not There: The Muses

Zhao Yi-heng[1]

One wonders if poetry is analyzable. Our scholarly forerunners told us that they preferred to set it in between. Wording is analyzed, without which, a poem is not possible to read. Yet wording itself is not sufficient to help grasp the true meaning of a poem.

From this point of view, one may say that poetry is designed to be unintelligible. If I claimed that I understand all of Chuan Sha's poems thoroughly, that would not be true. If I said that I have understood his poetry and that I am the most qualified person to review his book, I would sound lunatic. Confucius said, "If I do not have those to teach who rightly steer their course in the Middle Way, I would have to accept either the impetuous or the cautious ones. An impetuous man proceeds to possess, while a cautious man chooses to have something undone." If I cannot choose to be the cautious, I have to act impetuously. Yet, even with an aggressive intention, am I right set to obtain anything?

There seems to be, therefore, only one way left to solve the problem: to act as if I were impetuous. I do not mean to pretend to be an expert on something I have little

---

[1] Zhao Yi-heng, PhD (in comparative literature), is a London-based professor, writer, poet, and literary critic. He has published more than ten monographs and many literary works, among others.

knowledge of. What I mean is that I am bold enough to act as a specialist. In other words, I am writing something about which I feel rather clumsy. Am I sane to do so? The answer is yes, as there is no other way more justifiable. Poetry itself is actually an effort the poet exercises to look into a mystery, a trial to surpass the language limit from within, and an attempt to obtain something, be it analyzable or not.

As the saying goes, there is no need for one's heart to respond, for the language used in communication may continue in silence. Truth exists either beyond the text, or between the words, and it is beckoning just from where the poet stops. Silence speaks more, simply because the words may fail to meet the challenge.

Chuan Sha's poetry does not give us specific meanings, but it offers us a way to play with the meanings, a promise set seemingly to be realized. In my opinion, this explains why a poem is called a poem.

I believe it is appropriate to say that many of Chuan Sha's poems resemble games, albeit extremely serious games which grab your throat rather than offer you something pleasant in an adorable context. You may, as a result, feel a thrill of pleasure of being choked as well as a piercing pain. Even when your body and soul have come to the verge of a collapse, you still have the feeling that you will survive despite the near suffocation. Only at such a moment will the reader understand the real meaning of his words.

I can tell that Mr. Chuan Sha was seized from time to time by a sudden strike of consciousness in his writing, but I am not sure if I would have felt the same, or if other readers would. However, if we try, we will sooner or later catch the Muses, with their shifting eyes. We will then be freed from the daily boring routines, and be blessed.

2004
London, England

Acknowledgements

These poems, written in North America and Europe, first appeared in *Global Chinese Weekly* and *North American Times* in Canada. For fifteen months between early 2004 and mid 2005, one beautifully illustrated poem was printed weekly with its English translation in the *North American Times*. The English version was more appealing among native intellectuals, including college and university faculty members. They immediately and willingly offered advice in terms of language, so that the texts would have greater idiomatic value. As a result, the poems are as significant in China as they are beyond its boundaries.

I would like to express my heartfelt thanks to Mr. Hong Liu, the English translator who from the very start poured his talent into this difficult project. His unique and graceful style, with his delicately insightful traits of the true meanings, presents a masterpiece in the translation itself. This collection would have been quite different without him. I would also like to thank Professor Harry J. Huang for his substantial editorial input that made a real difference in this book. I truly appreciate every effort Bestview Scholars Publishing has made in publishing my poetry book in such a timely fashion. Thanks also go to Mr. Luo Fu, beloved poet and calligrapher from Taiwan, who wrote the Chinese title for a previous bilingual version of this book, the English text of which has been revised in part and edited by Bestview Scholars Publishing and published in the current edition. Artist Mr. Wang Wei-jun deserves my special thanks, for his artistic illustrations have added charm my poems printed in the *North American Times*. I would also thank Ms. Lo Lan, the art editor and designer. These three friends worked together to make the work a real piece of art for my Canadian readers.

Furthermore, I would like to thank the following friends who have helped bring this book into existence. They are: Mr. Ha Jin, Chinese-American writer, Dr. Luo Hui, translator, and Ms. Roo Borson and Mr. Kim Maltman, both Canadian poets. Mr. Qi Guang, Dean of Canadian Film Institute, who successfully led his team that performed my musical *Songs of Skirts* on stage. The Chinese-Canadian Poets Association and several local television and broadcasting corporations and dance schools joined forces and made the performance possible. I would like to thank these leading figures: Ms. Lin Yin (actress), Mr. Cheng Lu-yu (singer), Mr. Yu Xi (novelist), and the following performers: Ms. Qi Shu-juan, Ms. Wei Yin, Ms. Juan Zi, Ms. Lin Nan, Ms. Wang Yue, Ms. Chen Qi-tao, Ms. Ma Kai-lin, Ms. Yu Li-li, Ms. Zhang Xin, Ms Zhou Rui, Ms. Ma Mei-lin, Mr. Jin Dong, Mr. Guo Ran, Mr. Zhang Han-yuan, Mr. Huang Zheng, Mr. Fu Lei, Mr. Xun Yan, Ms. Tao Sun, Mr. Chen Gong, Ms. Zhang Hong, Ms. Du Li, and Ms. Qi Sha-ling.

I am grateful to many other unknown friends too. In their friendship, in their understanding of my work, and in their creative performances, I have found the beauty and glory of life. I will always remember them with gratitude.

Chuan Sha
2019

Chuan Sha's Literary Career

Chuan Sha, a Chinese-Canadian writer, poet, and playwright, was born in Chongqing in Sichuan, China, though his ancestral home is in Shandong. He enjoys the popularity of his versatile works, including novels, short stories, poems, plays, essays and literary reviews in the overseas Chinese literary community. A graduate of Sichuan University, Chuan Sha worked his way from an associate editor up to an editor-in-chief for a literary magazine for some years before pursuing further studies in the United Kingdom in 1991. He and his family immigrated to Canada in 1999.

Chuan Sha was Editor-in-Chief of Canada's Poseidon Publishing House, *Immigrants' World* (Journal), and Associate Editor-in-Chief of several newspapers including *North America Weekly*, *Global Chinese Press* (East Canada), and *Easyca*. Chuan Sha is presently the Director of the Chinese-Canadian Poets Association, a member of the Chinese PEN Society of Canada, Cultural Advisor to the Ontario Society of Chinese Education, the President and Vice Director of Da Ya Culture International Inc., Co-Chair of the General Committee of the International Da Ya Feng Prize for Literature, Executive Chair of the Evaluation Committee of the International Da Ya Feng Prize for Literature, Executive Chair of the North American Pacific Art Global League, Editor-in-Chief of http://pacificartsinfo.com, and Member of the Screenplay Evaluation Committee of the Canada-China International Film Festival (CCIFF).

Chuan Sha's major publications

The Shadowy Crowds (Poetry). China's Writers Press, 2001.

The Sojourners (Short Stories, Co-authored). Taiwan Buffalo Publishing House, 2004.

Sunlight (A novel). Taiwan Commercial Press, Ltd., 2004.

Spring Night (Poetry, in Chinese and English). Guangxi Normal University Press, 2006.

The Lady in the Blue-Flowered Mandarin Gown (A novel). Hua Shan Literature and Arts Press, 2012.

Language for a New Century: Contemporary Poetry from the Middle East, Asia, and Beyond (Included in the collection). New York: W. W. Norton & Company, 2007.

Variety Crossing Vol. 8 (Included in the collection) Toronto: Korean-Canadian Literary Forum-21 Press, 2006.

Skirts Are Singing (Poetry in 3-Act Musical). Three performances in O.I.S.E. Theatre, University of Toronto, 2004; York Woods Public Library Theatre, 2005; and Canada National TV Studio, 2013.

Harmony (Poetry in 5-Act Choir). Public performance given in the P.C. Ho Theatre on November 1, 2008.

Sunlight (2-Act Dance, based on the novel with the same name). Public performance given in Canada National TV Studio, September 2015.

Appreciation: Selected Poems by Chuan Sha (Critic Reviews). Chief Compiler: Li Yongyin, Assistant Compilers: Li Zhixiong, Fan Yun, and Hu Xiaogen. Hebei Education Press, 2010.

About the Translator

Hong Liu, Canadian freelance translator, was an Associate Professor of English in Guangxi Normal University in Guilin, China. He also taught Chinese (1995–1999) at Wake Forest University in Winston-Salem, North Carolina. His Chinese-English translation of *Untitled Lyrics*, a poetry anthology by Mr. Zhanqiu Liu, was published in 1994 by Hong Kong Literary Press. Mr. Liu lives in Ontario, Canada with his wife and daughter.

www.ingramcontent.com/pod-product-compliance
Lightning Source LLC
Chambersburg PA
CBHW030241170426
43202CB00027B/82